Unlocking Google's Evergreen Algorithms: Mastering SEO Strategies for Lasting Online Success

Welcome to "Unlocking Google's Evergreen Algorithms: Mastering SEO Strategies for Lasting Online Success." In this book, we delve into the fascinating world of Google's evergreen algorithms and explore the secrets behind achieving sustainable search engine optimization (SEO) results. As the digital landscape evolves, it is crucial for businesses and website owners to understand and adapt to these algorithms to maintain their online presence and thrive in the competitive online space.

Google's evergreen algorithms form the foundation of its search engine and determine how websites are ranked in search results. Unlike temporary algorithm updates, evergreen algorithms focus on long-term relevance and user satisfaction. They reward websites that consistently provide high-quality, valuable content and a seamless user experience.

Throughout this book, we will unravel the mysteries surrounding these evergreen algorithms, starting with an exploration of their core components, such as Google Panda, Penguin, Hummingbird, RankBrain, and BERT. We will examine how each algorithm works and the specific factors they prioritize when evaluating websites.

But understanding the algorithms is just the beginning. We will guide you through practical strategies and techniques for creating evergreen content, building authoritative backlinks, optimizing your website for on-page SEO, and enhancing user experience and engagement. You will gain insights into the latest trends, such as mobile optimization, voice search, and the role of artificial intelligence in shaping the future of search.

This book goes beyond theory; it offers actionable advice, real-world case studies, and expert tips to help you unlock the full potential of Google's evergreen algorithms. Whether you are a business owner, marketer, SEO professional, or website administrator, this comprehensive guide will equip you with the knowledge and tools you need to master SEO strategies for lasting online success.

So, let's embark on this exciting journey together and uncover the key to unlocking Google's evergreen algorithms and achieving sustainable SEO results.

I. Introduction to Google's Evergreen Algorithms

Understanding The Concept Of Evergreen Algorithms

Evergreen algorithms, in the context of search engines, refer to the core algorithms and ranking factors that remain relatively stable and consistent over time. Unlike specific algorithm updates or changes, which can have significant and immediate impacts on search rankings, evergreen algorithms are the foundation upon which search engines operate.

The term "evergreen" suggests that these algorithms retain their relevance and effectiveness over the long term, regardless of the evolving nature of search engine technology and user behavior. While search engines like Google regularly update and refine their algorithms, the fundamental principles behind how search results are determined tend to remain consistent.

Evergreen algorithms focus on delivering the most relevant and valuable content to users based on their search queries. They consider a variety of factors, including keyword relevance, website authority, user engagement, and overall content quality. By relying on these core principles, search engines aim to provide users with the most accurate and useful search results.

Understanding evergreen algorithms is essential for anyone involved in search engine optimization (SEO) and content creation. It means focusing on creating high-quality, informative, and user-friendly content that aligns with the intent of search queries. It also emphasizes the importance of building a strong website authority through quality backlinks and positive user experiences.

While evergreen algorithms provide a stable foundation, it's crucial to stay informed about algorithm updates and changes. Although the core principles may not drastically shift, search engines continually refine their algorithms to deliver better search experiences. Staying updated allows SEO practitioners to adapt their strategies and ensure their content remains optimized for search visibility.

In summary, evergreen algorithms form the backbone of search engine operations, focusing on delivering relevant and valuable content to users. By understanding these core principles and incorporating them into your SEO strategies, you can enhance your website's visibility and provide a better user experience.

Importance Of Evergreen Content For Sustainable Seo

Evergreen content plays a crucial role in sustainable SEO (Search Engine Optimization) strategies. It refers to content that remains relevant and valuable to readers over an extended period, standing the test of time regardless of changing trends or events. Here are some reasons why evergreen content is essential for sustainable SEO:

Long-Term Relevance: Evergreen content addresses timeless topics and provides information that remains relevant for an extended period. It continues to attract organic traffic and generate interest from users long after it's published. This longevity helps in maintaining a consistent flow of traffic to your website.

Increased Search Visibility: Search engines value evergreen content because it aligns with their goal of providing users with relevant and useful information. Such content tends to rank higher in search engine results over time, increasing your website's visibility and attracting organic traffic.

Sustainable Traffic Generation: Unlike time-sensitive content that experiences spikes in traffic during specific periods, evergreen content consistently generates traffic over the long term. It acts as a valuable asset for your website, continuously attracting new visitors and maintaining a steady flow of organic traffic.

Builds Website Authority: Evergreen content helps establish your website as a reliable and authoritative source of information within your niche. As users find your content valuable and share it, you earn backlinks, social shares, and references from other websites. This, in turn, boosts your website's authority and credibility, leading to higher search engine rankings.

Supports Internal Linking: Evergreen content provides an opportunity for internal linking within your website. By strategically linking to relevant evergreen articles from newer content, you can enhance the SEO value of both the new and existing pages. This internal linking structure improves user navigation and helps search engines crawl and index your website more effectively.

Evergreen Content Updates: While evergreen content remains relevant for a long time, it's important to periodically review and update it to ensure accuracy and freshness. By refreshing the content, you demonstrate your commitment to providing up-to-date and reliable information, which positively impacts your SEO efforts.

Incorporating evergreen content into your SEO strategy helps you build a strong foundation for long-term success. By consistently creating and optimizing valuable content that stands the test of time, you can attract organic traffic, enhance search visibility, and establish your website as an authoritative source within your industry.

II. Exploring the Core Evergreen Algorithms

Google Panda: Content Quality And User Engagement

Google Panda is a search algorithm update introduced by Google in 2011, with subsequent updates and refinements over the years. It focuses on evaluating the quality of website content and its overall user engagement. The primary goal of Google Panda is to ensure that high-quality and relevant content ranks higher in search engine results while penalizing websites with low-quality or thin content.

The main factors that Google Panda considers when evaluating content quality and user engagement are:

Content Relevance: Panda looks at how well the content matches the search queries and user intent. Websites that provide comprehensive, accurate, and relevant information are favored.

Content Quality: Panda assesses the overall quality of the content, including factors such as originality, depth, and uniqueness. Websites with well-researched, informative, and valuable content tend to rank higher.

Thin or Low-Quality Content: Panda penalizes websites with thin or low-quality content, such as pages with little to no substantial content, keyword stuffing, or excessive advertising. Websites with such content may experience a drop in rankings.

User Engagement Metrics: Panda considers user engagement metrics, such as bounce rate, time on site, and page views per visit, to gauge how users interact with the content. Websites with high user engagement tend to rank better, as it indicates that the content is valuable and engaging.

Site Usability and User Experience: Panda also evaluates the overall usability and user experience of a website. Factors such as page load speed, mobile-friendliness, ease of navigation, and overall website design impact rankings.

To ensure that your website is not adversely affected by Google Panda and to improve your SEO performance, here are some best practices to follow:

Create High-Quality Content: Focus on creating unique, comprehensive, and valuable content that meets the needs of your target audience. Conduct thorough research, provide in-depth information, and ensure your content is well-written and engaging.

Avoid Thin or Duplicate Content: Remove or improve any thin or duplicate content on your website. Consolidate similar pages, rewrite thin content, and ensure each page offers unique and valuable information.

Enhance User Engagement: Improve user engagement metrics by optimizing your website's design, navigation, and overall user experience. Make sure your content is easy to read, visually appealing, and encourages users to stay on your website longer.

Optimize Site Performance: Ensure your website loads quickly, is mobile-friendly, and provides a seamless user experience across different devices. Optimize images, minimize code, and utilize caching and content delivery networks (CDNs) to improve page speed.

Monitor Analytics: Regularly monitor your website analytics to track user engagement metrics, identify areas for improvement, and address any issues that may impact your SEO performance.

By focusing on content quality, user engagement, and overall site optimization, you can align your website with the goals of Google Panda and improve your chances of ranking higher in search engine results.

Google Penguin: Link Quality And Spam Prevention

Google Penguin is a search algorithm update introduced by Google in 2012, designed to target and penalize websites that engage in manipulative link building practices and violate Google's Webmaster Guidelines. The primary focus of Google Penguin is to evaluate the quality and relevance of a website's backlink profile to ensure a more reliable and spam-free search experience for users.

Here are the key aspects of Google Penguin related to link quality and spam prevention:

Link Quality Assessment: Penguin algorithm assesses the quality of backlinks pointing to a website. It examines factors such as the relevance, authority, and naturalness of the links. Websites with high-quality, relevant, and organic backlinks tend to rank better in search results.

Link Spam Detection: Penguin algorithm identifies and penalizes websites that employ link schemes, such as buying or selling links, participating in link farms, or engaging in excessive link exchanges. These spammy link practices are seen as manipulative attempts to manipulate search rankings and are strongly discouraged by Google.

Anchor Text Optimization: Penguin looks at the anchor text used in backlinks to determine its relevance and naturalness. Over-optimized anchor text, where the same keyword is used excessively, is considered a red flag and may result in penalties. It's important to maintain a diverse and natural anchor text profile.

Disavow Tool: Google provides a Disavow Tool that allows website owners to request the exclusion of specific backlinks from their link profile. This tool can be used to disassociate from low-quality or spammy links pointing to a website.

Link Building Best Practices: To align with Google Penguin and build a strong and sustainable backlink profile, focus on acquiring high-quality and relevant backlinks through legitimate means. This includes creating valuable content that naturally attracts links, guest blogging on reputable websites, building relationships with influencers, and engaging in content marketing and outreach efforts.

It's crucial to prioritize link quality and adhere to ethical link building practices to avoid penalties from Google Penguin. Here are some best practices:

- Focus on earning organic and natural backlinks through high-quality content and valuable resources.
- Conduct regular backlink audits to identify and address any potentially harmful or low-quality links.
- Disavow any spammy or irrelevant links using Google's Disavow Tool if necessary.
- Build relationships with authoritative websites and influencers in your industry to secure relevant and valuable backlinks.
- Monitor your backlink profile and respond promptly to any suspicious or unwanted links.

By maintaining a strong focus on link quality, avoiding manipulative practices, and consistently improving your website's backlink profile, you can safeguard your website from penalties and improve your overall SEO performance.

Google Hummingbird: Semantic Search And Context Understanding

Google Hummingbird is a major search algorithm update introduced by Google in 2013. Unlike previous algorithm updates that primarily focused on specific aspects of search, Hummingbird aimed to bring about a fundamental shift in how search results are delivered by emphasizing semantic search and context understanding.

Here are the key aspects of Google Hummingbird related to semantic search and context understanding:

Semantic Search: Hummingbird introduced a deeper understanding of the meaning behind search queries and web content. It aims to provide more relevant search results by interpreting the intent of the user rather than just matching keywords. This means that Google can better understand the context and relationships between words, allowing for more accurate search results.

Natural Language Processing: Hummingbird improved Google's ability to understand natural language queries and conversational search. It takes into account the entire search query, rather than focusing solely on individual keywords, and aims to deliver results that best match the user's query, even if the exact words aren't used.

Knowledge Graph Integration: Hummingbird integrates with Google's Knowledge Graph, which is a vast database of interconnected information about people, places, and things. By understanding the relationships between entities, Hummingbird can provide more comprehensive and relevant search results that go beyond simple keyword matching.

Long-Tail Keyword Optimization: With Hummingbird, there is a greater emphasis on optimizing for long-tail keywords and conversational phrases. Websites that provide detailed, informative content that addresses specific queries have a better chance of ranking well in search results.

Contextual Understanding: Hummingbird takes into account the user's search history, location, and other relevant factors to provide personalized and contextually relevant search results. This allows Google to deliver more tailored and meaningful results based on the user's specific needs.

To adapt to Google Hummingbird and optimize for semantic search and context understanding, consider the following best practices:

- Focus on creating high-quality, comprehensive content that addresses specific topics and provides valuable information.
- Incorporate long-tail keywords and conversational phrases naturally within your content.
- Use structured data markup to provide additional context to search engines and enhance the visibility of your content in rich snippets.
- Aim to answer questions and provide solutions to user queries in a clear and concise manner.
- Understand the intent behind different search queries and create content that aligns with those intents.
- Monitor and analyze your website's performance in search results, identifying areas where you can improve the relevance and contextuality of your content.

By embracing semantic search and context understanding, you can align your website with Google Hummingbird and improve your chances of delivering highly relevant and meaningful content to your audience.

Google Rankbrain: Machine Learning And Search Relevance

Google RankBrain is a machine learning-based algorithm introduced by Google in 2015. It is designed to enhance the search engine's understanding of complex search queries and improve search results' relevance. RankBrain uses artificial intelligence and natural language processing techniques to interpret and learn from user queries, helping Google provide more accurate and meaningful search results.

Here are the key aspects of Google RankBrain related to machine learning and search relevance:

Interpreting User Queries: RankBrain focuses on understanding the context and intent behind search queries, particularly those that are ambiguous or lack clear keyword matches. It analyzes various factors, such as the words used, the search history, and the searcher's location, to provide the most relevant results.

Learning from User Behavior: RankBrain continuously learns and improves over time by analyzing how users interact with search results. It pays attention to metrics like click-through rates, dwell time (the amount of time spent on a page after clicking from the search results), and bounce rates to assess the relevance and quality of search results.

Handling Unfamiliar Queries: RankBrain is especially useful for handling queries it hasn't encountered before. By leveraging its machine learning capabilities, it can make educated guesses about the user's intent and provide relevant results based on similar past queries.

Enhancing Search Results: RankBrain influences the ranking of search results by determining which pages are more likely to be relevant to a particular query. It helps Google understand the content of web pages better and match them to user queries based on their underlying meaning rather than relying solely on keyword matches.

To optimize for Google RankBrain and improve search relevance, consider the following best practices:

- Focus on user intent: Create content that aligns with the searcher's intent and provides valuable information that satisfies their needs.
- Use natural language: Optimize your content with conversational and long-tail keywords that reflect how users phrase their queries.
- Provide comprehensive content: Create in-depth and authoritative content that covers the topic thoroughly, answering potential questions and addressing related subtopics.
- Improve user experience: Ensure your website is user-friendly, loads quickly, and provides a seamless experience across devices.
- Monitor and analyze user behavior metrics: Track metrics like click-through rates, bounce rates, and dwell time to gain insights into how users engage with your content and make improvements accordingly.

By understanding Google RankBrain's role in machine learning and search relevance, you can adapt your SEO strategies to provide more meaningful and valuable content that aligns with user intent, ultimately improving your website's visibility and attracting relevant organic traffic.

Google Bert: Natural Language Processing And Understanding

Google BERT (Bidirectional Encoder Representations from Transformers) is a natural language processing (NLP) model introduced by Google in 2019. It aims to improve the search engine's ability to understand the context and meaning of words in a sentence by considering the surrounding words and their relationship with each other.

Here are the key aspects of Google BERT related to natural language processing and understanding:

Contextual Understanding: BERT focuses on understanding the nuances of language by considering the full context of a word within a sentence. It takes into account the words that come before and after it to grasp the intended meaning and context.

Pre-training and Fine-tuning: BERT is pre-trained on a large corpus of text data to learn the relationships between words. It uses a transformer architecture, which allows it to capture long-range dependencies and understand the context of words in a sentence. After pre-training, BERT is fine-tuned on specific tasks, such as question answering or text classification, to make it more effective for those particular applications.

Handling Ambiguity: BERT is particularly helpful in resolving ambiguous queries or phrases where the meaning can change based on the context. By considering the entire sentence and the relationships between words, BERT can provide more accurate and relevant search results.

Multilingual Support: BERT has been trained on data from multiple languages, enabling it to understand and process text in different languages effectively. This improves search results for users across various regions and languages.

To optimize your content for Google BERT and enhance natural language processing, consider the following best practices:

- Focus on user intent: Craft your content to match the specific intent behind user queries. Understand the context and meaning of the keywords and phrases being used.
- Write in natural language: Create content that uses conversational and natural language patterns. BERT can better understand and interpret content that mimics human conversation.
- Provide comprehensive answers: Ensure that your content provides thorough and relevant answers to user queries. Address common questions and provide in-depth information to satisfy user intent.
- Use diverse language: Incorporate a variety of language patterns and synonyms related to your topic. This helps BERT understand the context better and improves the relevance of your content.
- Regularly review and update your content: BERT continuously learns and adapts to language patterns. Stay updated with algorithm changes and periodically review and update your content to ensure it remains relevant and optimized for BERT.

By understanding the role of Google BERT in natural language processing and understanding, you can optimize your content to align with user intent, provide meaningful answers, and improve the visibility and ranking of your website in search results.

III. Creating Evergreen Content

Identifying Evergreen Topics And Keywords

Identifying evergreen topics and keywords is essential for creating content that remains relevant and valuable to your audience over time. Here are some strategies to help you identify evergreen topics and keywords:

Understand your audience: Start by understanding your target audience's needs, interests, and pain points. What topics are they consistently interested in? What questions do they frequently ask? This will give you insight into the types of evergreen content that will resonate with them.

Conduct keyword research: Use keyword research tools like Google Keyword Planner, SEMrush, or Ahrefs to identify keywords with consistent search volume over time. Look for keywords that are related to your niche and have a high search volume and low competition. These keywords often indicate evergreen topics.

Look for timeless concepts and principles: Evergreen content is often based on timeless concepts and principles that remain relevant regardless of current trends. Examples include "How to Lose Weight," "Tips for Financial Planning," or "Effective Communication Skills." These topics will likely have enduring value and attract consistent interest.

Consider beginner-level content: Beginner-level content tends to be evergreen as it caters to newcomers in a particular field or topic. Beginners will always exist, so creating content that educates and guides them can be valuable over the long term.

Monitor industry trends and news: While evergreen content focuses on timeless topics, it's also important to stay updated on industry trends and news. By combining evergreen topics with timely information, you can create content that remains relevant even as the industry evolves.

Explore FAQs and common problems: Frequently Asked Questions (FAQs) and common problems are excellent sources of evergreen content ideas. Identify the questions or challenges that your audience regularly encounters, and create comprehensive content that provides solutions and guidance.

Analyze competitor's evergreen content: Study your competitors' websites and blogs to identify their evergreen content. Look for topics that consistently attract engagement, social shares, and backlinks. While you should never copy their content, analyzing their successful evergreen topics can inspire your own ideas.

Remember, evergreen topics are not limited to specific industries. They can exist in various niches, such as health, finance, lifestyle, or personal development. The key is to find subjects that have enduring relevance and can provide value to your audience consistently.

Crafting High-Quality, In-Depth Articles And Guides

Crafting high-quality, in-depth articles and guides is crucial for creating evergreen content that provides value to your audience and establishes your authority in the field. Here are some tips to help you create such content:

Conduct thorough research: Before writing your article or guide, gather information from reliable sources such as reputable websites, industry reports, books, and scholarly articles. Ensure that your content is based on accurate and up-to-date information.

Outline your content: Create a well-structured outline that outlines the main sections and subtopics you will cover. This will help you maintain a logical flow and ensure that you cover all the necessary points.

Provide comprehensive information: Dive deep into the topic and provide in-depth information. Avoid superficial or generic content. Your readers should walk away with a thorough understanding of the subject and practical insights they can apply.

Use a conversational tone: Write in a conversational tone that engages your readers and makes the content more relatable. Avoid using jargon or technical terms without explaining them. Aim to strike a balance between professionalism and approachability.

Break down complex concepts: If you're discussing complex concepts or processes, break them down into simpler, digestible chunks. Use examples, analogies, and visuals to help readers grasp the information more easily.

Include visuals and multimedia: Incorporate relevant visuals such as images, infographics, charts, or videos to enhance the readability and understanding of your content. Visuals can break up the text and make it more engaging.

Back up your claims with evidence: When making assertions or presenting facts, support them with credible sources or data. This adds credibility to your content and builds trust with your audience.

Use subheadings and bullet points: Organize your content using subheadings and bullet points to make it scannable. This allows readers to quickly navigate through the article and find the information they need.

Optimize for readability and SEO: Use short paragraphs, clear and concise sentences, and appropriate headings to improve readability. Incorporate relevant keywords naturally throughout the content to optimize it for search engines.

Edit and proofread: Before publishing, thoroughly edit and proofread your content to eliminate grammatical errors, typos, and inconsistencies. Consider asking a trusted colleague or friend to review your work for an additional perspective.

Remember, high-quality, in-depth content takes time and effort to create. Focus on providing value to your readers, addressing their pain points, and delivering information that is actionable and relevant. By crafting comprehensive and well-researched articles and guides, you can establish yourself as a trusted source of information and attract a loyal audience.

Optimizing Content For User Intent And Search Queries

Optimizing content for user intent and search queries is crucial for ensuring that your content aligns with what users are looking for and improving its visibility in search engine results. Here are some strategies to optimize your content for user intent and search queries:

Understand user intent: User intent refers to the underlying purpose or goal behind a user's search query. It can be informational (seeking information), navigational (looking for a specific website or page), transactional (aiming to make a purchase), or commercial (researching products or services). Understand the intent behind the keywords you target and create content that fulfills that intent.

Conduct keyword research: Use keyword research tools to identify relevant keywords and phrases that align with user intent. Look for keywords with high search volume and relevance to your content. Consider long-tail keywords that are more specific and reflect user intent more accurately.

Analyze search engine results pages (SERPs): Examine the search results for your target keywords to understand the types of content that rank well. Look for patterns in the content format, structure, and information provided. This will give you insights into the content that best satisfies user intent.

Create valuable and comprehensive content: Craft your content to provide valuable and relevant information that satisfies user intent. Address common questions and concerns related to the topic and provide comprehensive answers. Use subheadings, bullet points, and visual elements to make the content easily scannable and digestible.

Optimize title tags and meta descriptions: Craft compelling title tags and meta descriptions that accurately describe the content and entice users to click. Incorporate relevant keywords naturally while ensuring the information is clear and enticing.

Use structured data markup: Implement structured data markup, such as schema.org, to provide additional context to search engines about the content of your page. This can help search engines understand and present your content in a more meaningful way in the search results.

Monitor and analyze user behavior: Use analytics tools to track user behavior on your website, including metrics like bounce rate, time on page, and conversion rates. Analyze this data to understand how well your content is meeting user intent and making necessary improvements based on user feedback.

Continuously optimize and update your content: Regularly review and update your content to ensure it remains relevant and valuable over time. Keep up with changes in user intent and search trends and adapt your content accordingly. Monitor keyword performance and make adjustments as needed.

Remember, optimizing your content for user intent and search queries is an ongoing process. Stay informed about your target audience, their search behavior, and emerging trends in your industry. By aligning your content with user intent and providing valuable information, you can improve your visibility in search results and drive organic traffic to your website.

Incorporating Multimedia Elements For Enhanced Engagement

Incorporating multimedia elements in your content can greatly enhance user engagement and provide a richer and more immersive experience for your audience. Here are some tips for effectively incorporating multimedia elements:

Images and Graphics: Include relevant and high-quality images and graphics that complement your content. Visuals can help break up text, make your content more visually appealing, and convey information more effectively. Use images to illustrate concepts, provide examples, or evoke emotions related to your topic.

Infographics: Create informative and visually appealing infographics that present data, statistics, or complex information in a concise and easy-to-understand format. Infographics are highly shareable and can attract more attention and engagement on social media platforms.

Videos: Embed videos in your content to provide dynamic and engaging visual content. You can create tutorial videos, product demonstrations, interviews, or animated explainer videos to enhance understanding and engage your audience. Host your videos on platforms like YouTube or Vimeo and embed them on your website or blog.

Slideshows and Presentations: Use slideshows or presentations to present information in a visually engaging manner. Platforms like SlideShare allow you to upload and share slideshows, enabling you to reach a wider audience and drive traffic back to your website.

Audio Content: Consider incorporating audio elements such as podcasts or recorded interviews to provide an alternative format for your audience to consume your content. Audio content is convenient for on-the-go listening and can help you connect with audiences who prefer auditory learning.

Interactive Elements: Add interactive elements like quizzes, polls, surveys, or interactive charts and graphs to actively engage your audience. These elements encourage participation and make the content more interactive and memorable.

Social Media Integration: Encourage users to share your multimedia content on social media platforms by providing social sharing buttons. This can increase the visibility and reach of your content, driving more engagement and traffic to your website.

Accessibility Considerations: Ensure that your multimedia elements are accessible to all users, including those with visual or hearing impairments. Provide alternative text descriptions for images, transcripts for videos or audio content, and ensure that any interactive elements are compatible with assistive technologies.

Remember, when incorporating multimedia elements, it's essential to strike a balance and ensure they enhance your content rather than distract from it. Choose media that aligns with your content objectives and audience preferences. Additionally, optimize the file sizes and formats of your multimedia elements to maintain optimal website performance and loading speed.

Strategies For Updating And Refreshing Evergreen Content

Updating and refreshing evergreen content is crucial to maintain its relevance, accuracy, and value over time. Here are some strategies for effectively updating and refreshing your evergreen content:

Conduct Regular Content Audits: Schedule regular content audits to identify which evergreen pieces need updating. Assess the performance of your content, analyze user engagement metrics, and identify areas that require improvement or updating.

Update Statistical Data and Facts: Evergreen content often includes statistical data or facts. Keep these elements up to date by verifying the information and replacing outdated data with the latest and most accurate figures.

Refresh Examples and Case Studies: If your evergreen content includes examples or case studies, consider refreshing them with more recent and relevant examples. This helps to make your content more relatable and applicable to current scenarios.

Add New Information and Insights: Stay updated with industry trends, developments, and research related to your evergreen topic. Incorporate new information, insights, and perspectives into your content to ensure it remains valuable and informative.

Improve Formatting and Readability: Take the opportunity to enhance the formatting and readability of your evergreen content. Break up long paragraphs, use subheadings, bullet points, and numbered lists to make the content easier to scan and digest. Additionally, consider optimizing the content for mobile devices to cater to the increasing number of mobile users.

Enhance Visual Elements: Update and enhance the visual elements within your evergreen content. Replace outdated or low-quality images with high-resolution, relevant visuals. Consider adding new infographics, charts, or illustrations to improve the visual appeal and comprehension of your content.

Incorporate User Feedback: Pay attention to user feedback and comments on your evergreen content. Address any questions, suggestions, or concerns raised by your audience. Use their feedback to identify areas for improvement and to provide further clarity or insights.

Link to Updated Resources: If you come across new and valuable resources related to your evergreen topic, incorporate them into your content and provide relevant links. This demonstrates your commitment to staying current and provides readers with additional sources of information.

Promote the Updated Content: Once you've updated and refreshed your evergreen content, don't forget to promote it. Share the updated content on your website, social media channels, and newsletters. Reach out to relevant influencers or industry websites to let them know about the updated version.

By consistently updating and refreshing your evergreen content, you can maintain its relevance, boost its search engine visibility, and continue to provide value to your audience over time.

IV. Building Authoritative Backlinks

Understanding The Role Of Backlinks In Seo

Backlinks play a crucial role in search engine optimization (SEO) as they are a significant factor in determining the credibility, authority, and visibility of a website. A backlink is a link from another website that points back to your website. Search engines like Google consider backlinks as votes of confidence from other websites, indicating that your content is valuable and trustworthy. Here are key points to understand about the role of backlinks in SEO:

Authority and Trust: Backlinks act as endorsements or references from other websites, signaling to search engines that your website is authoritative and trustworthy. Websites with a strong backlink profile tend to rank higher in search engine results pages (SERPs).

Improved Organic Rankings: Search engines analyze the quality and quantity of backlinks to determine the relevance and authority of a website. Websites with high-quality backlinks from reputable sources are more likely to rank higher in organic search results.

Referral Traffic: Backlinks not only enhance your website's visibility in search results but also generate referral traffic. When users click on a backlink from another website, they are directed to your website, increasing the chances of engagement, conversions, and leads.

Link Diversity: Having a diverse portfolio of backlinks from various sources, such as industry publications, reputable blogs, social media platforms, and directories, helps establish your website's credibility. A diverse range of backlinks indicates that your website is valued by different online communities and enhances your overall SEO strategy.

Anchor Text Optimization: Backlinks often contain anchor text, which is the clickable text that users see. Optimizing anchor text with relevant keywords helps search engines understand the context and relevance of the linked page. However, it's important to maintain a natural balance and avoid over-optimization, as search engines penalize manipulative practices.

Natural Link Building: Focus on building natural, organic backlinks rather than engaging in manipulative tactics. Natural link building occurs when other websites voluntarily link to your content because they find it valuable and informative. High-quality content, guest blogging, influencer outreach, and networking within your industry are effective strategies for earning natural backlinks.

Quality Over Quantity: While the number of backlinks is important, the quality of those backlinks matters more. A few high-quality backlinks from authoritative websites can have a greater impact on your SEO than numerous low-quality backlinks. Focus on acquiring backlinks from reputable sources that are relevant to your industry or niche.

Monitoring and Disavowing: Regularly monitor your backlink profile to identify any low-quality or spammy backlinks that could negatively impact your SEO. If you come across harmful backlinks, you can use the Google Disavow tool to ask search engines not to consider those links when assessing your website.

Building a strong backlink profile takes time and effort. It requires creating valuable content, fostering relationships with influencers and industry peers, and actively promoting your website. By earning high-quality backlinks, you can improve your website's authority, visibility, and organic rankings in search engine results.

Techniques For Acquiring High-Quality, Relevant Backlinks

Acquiring high-quality, relevant backlinks is an essential aspect of an effective SEO strategy. Here are some techniques you can use to acquire such backlinks:

Create Outstanding Content: One of the most effective ways to attract backlinks is by creating high-quality, valuable content. When you publish content that is informative, unique, and engaging, other websites and bloggers are more likely to link to it as a valuable resource.

Guest Blogging: Guest blogging involves writing and publishing articles on other websites within your industry or niche. By contributing valuable content to reputable websites, you can earn backlinks in return. Make sure to choose websites that have a good reputation and align with your target audience.

Influencer Outreach: Identify influencers or experts in your industry and establish relationships with them. Collaborate on content projects or ask them to review your products or services. When influencers mention or link to your website, it can generate high-quality backlinks and increase your credibility.

Broken Link Building: Find websites in your industry that have broken links, i.e., links that lead to non-existent pages. Reach out to the website owner and suggest replacing the broken link with a link to a relevant page on your website. This technique provides value to the website owner by helping them fix broken links while earning you a backlink.

Resource Link Building: Create comprehensive resource guides, tutorials, or tools that provide significant value to your target audience. Reach out to relevant websites, bloggers, and online communities that may find your resource helpful. If they find your content valuable, they may link to it as a reference for their own audience.

Social Media Promotion: Share your content on social media platforms to increase its visibility and reach. When people discover your content through social media, there is a chance they may link to it on their websites or share it with their followers.

Participate in Industry Forums and Communities: Engage in online forums and communities related to your industry. Contribute valuable insights and build relationships with fellow members. When appropriate, share links to your content if it adds value to the discussion. However, avoid spamming or self-promotion, as it may harm your reputation.

Create Infographics or Visual Content: Infographics and visual content are highly shareable and can attract backlinks from websites looking to provide visual content to their audience. Ensure your infographics are well-designed, contain valuable information, and include an embed code so that other websites can easily share them.

Build Relationships with Webmasters: Establish connections with website owners and webmasters in your industry. Engage in conversations, provide value, and offer assistance whenever possible. Building relationships can lead to opportunities for guest posting, collaborative projects, and natural backlink placements.

Monitor Your Competitors: Keep an eye on your competitors' backlink profiles and identify opportunities they may have missed. Look for websites that link to multiple competitors and reach out to them with a value proposition for linking to your website as well.

Remember, acquiring high-quality backlinks takes time and effort. Focus on building relationships, creating valuable content, and promoting your website in ethical ways. Building a strong backlink profile will improve your website's authority, visibility, and search engine rankings over time.

Guest Blogging And Influencer Outreach Strategies

Guest blogging and influencer outreach are two effective strategies for acquiring high-quality backlinks and increasing your online visibility. Here are some tips for implementing these strategies effectively:

Guest Blogging:

- Identify Relevant Websites: Research websites in your industry or niche that accept guest posts. Look for websites that have a good reputation, high domain authority, and a relevant audience. Make sure their content aligns with your expertise and target audience.
- Build Relationships: Before reaching out to websites, engage with them through comments, social media, or email. Establishing a relationship with the website owner or editor increases your chances of getting your guest post accepted.
- Create Compelling Pitches: When reaching out to website owners or editors, craft personalized and well-researched pitches. Highlight the value you can provide to their audience, suggest topic ideas, and showcase your expertise. Make it clear how your guest post aligns with their website's content and goals.
- Craft High-Quality Content: When writing your guest post, focus on delivering valuable and well-researched content. Provide unique insights, actionable tips, and engaging storytelling. Ensure that your content aligns with the website's guidelines and follows their formatting and style.
- Author Bio and Backlinks: Include a well-crafted author bio that highlights your expertise and includes a link back to your website or relevant content. Use anchor text strategically to optimize the backlink for SEO purposes.

Influencer Outreach:

- Identify Relevant Influencers: Research influencers in your industry or niche who have a significant following and engage with their audience. Look for influencers whose values and target audience align with your brand.
- Engage with Influencers: Before reaching out, engage with influencers by following them on social media, sharing their content, and leaving thoughtful comments. Building a genuine connection increases the chances of a positive response.
- Personalize Your Outreach: Craft personalized outreach messages that demonstrate your knowledge of the influencer's work and explain why you believe collaborating would be beneficial for both parties. Offer specific ideas or proposals for collaboration.
- Provide Value: Show how your collaboration can provide value to the influencer and their audience. Offer to create content, contribute to their blog, provide exclusive insights, or collaborate on a joint project. Emphasize the mutual benefits of the partnership.
- Maintain Relationships: After collaborating with an influencer, maintain the relationship by continuing to engage with their content, sharing their updates, and supporting their initiatives. Building long-term relationships with influencers can lead to ongoing opportunities for collaboration and backlink opportunities.

Remember, both guest blogging and influencer outreach require a genuine and value-driven approach. Focus on building relationships, providing valuable content, and offering mutual benefits. By leveraging the reach and credibility of established websites and influencers, you can acquire high-quality backlinks and increase your online visibility.

Building Relationships With Industry Experts And Thought Leaders

Building relationships with industry experts and thought leaders can be incredibly valuable for your SEO efforts. Here are some strategies to help you establish and nurture these relationships:

Research and Identify Key Players: Start by identifying the key experts and thought leaders in your industry or niche. Look for individuals who have a strong online presence, authoritative content, and a significant following. Pay attention to their expertise and the topics they cover.

Engage on Social Media: Follow these experts on social media platforms like Twitter, LinkedIn, and Facebook. Engage with their content by liking, sharing, and commenting on their posts. Offer insightful comments that demonstrate your knowledge and interest in their field.

Share Their Content: Help promote their content by sharing it with your audience. This shows your support and helps to increase their visibility. Tag them in your posts or use their social media handles to get their attention.

Leave Thoughtful Comments: When they publish blog posts or articles, make an effort to leave thoughtful comments that contribute to the conversation. Add value by sharing your insights, asking relevant questions, or offering additional resources. This helps you establish yourself as a knowledgeable and engaged member of the community.

Attend Industry Events: Look for conferences, webinars, and networking events where these experts are speaking or participating. Attend these events and actively engage with them during Q&A sessions, panel discussions, or networking opportunities. Introduce yourself and express your interest in their work.

Collaborate on Content: Seek opportunities to collaborate with industry experts on content projects. This could include co-authoring blog posts, conducting interviews, or hosting joint webinars or podcasts. Collaborative content not only strengthens your relationship with the expert but also exposes you to their audience, increasing your visibility.

Offer Your Expertise: If you have specialized knowledge or unique insights, offer to contribute guest articles or be a guest speaker on their platforms. Provide value by sharing your expertise and contributing to their audience's knowledge base.

Build Genuine Connections: Approach relationship-building with a genuine interest in the expert's work and a desire to establish meaningful connections. Avoid being overly promotional or self-centered in your interactions. Instead, focus on building mutual respect and trust.

Remember, building relationships takes time and effort. Be patient and consistent in your engagement. As you establish yourself as a valuable contributor and supporter, industry experts and thought leaders are more likely to recognize and appreciate your efforts. These relationships can lead to collaborative opportunities, backlinks, and increased visibility for your SEO efforts.

V. On-Page SEO Optimization for Evergreen Algorithms

Keyword Research And Optimization Techniques

Keyword research and optimization are crucial components of an effective SEO strategy. Here are some techniques to help you with keyword research and optimization:

Understand Your Audience: Start by understanding your target audience and their search intent. Identify the topics and keywords they are likely to use when searching for information related to your website or business. Put yourself in their shoes and think about what they would search for.

Use Keyword Research Tools: Utilize keyword research tools such as Google Keyword Planner, SEMrush, Ahrefs, or Moz Keyword Explorer to discover relevant keywords. These tools provide insights into keyword search volume, competition, and related keywords. Explore both short-tail and long-tail keywords to target a wider range of search queries.

Long-Tail Keywords: Long-tail keywords are longer and more specific keyword phrases. They often have less competition and can attract highly targeted traffic. Incorporate long-tail keywords into your content to capture niche audiences and increase your chances of ranking higher in search results.

Keyword Competition and Difficulty: Evaluate the competition and difficulty level of keywords. Focus on keywords with a good search volume but lower competition to increase your chances of ranking well. Long-tail keywords typically have lower competition and can be a great starting point.

On-Page Optimization: Once you have identified your target keywords, optimize your website's on-page elements. Include the target keyword in the page title, meta description, URL, headings (H1, H2, etc.), and throughout the content. However, make sure to maintain a natural flow and avoid keyword stuffing.

High-Quality Content: Create high-quality, informative, and relevant content that satisfies the user's search intent. Incorporate your target keywords naturally within the content, focusing on providing value to the reader. Well-written, engaging content that matches user intent is more likely to rank higher in search results.

Internal Linking: Implement internal linking strategies to connect relevant pages on your website. Linking between related content helps search engines understand the structure and relevance of your website. Use keyword-rich anchor text to optimize internal links.

Monitor and Refine: Continuously monitor your keyword rankings and performance using SEO analytics tools. Regularly review and refine your keyword strategy based on data insights. Identify opportunities to optimize underperforming pages or target new keywords based on emerging trends.

Remember, SEO is an ongoing process, and keyword research and optimization should be regularly revisited and refined. Keep up with industry trends, user behavior, and search engine algorithm changes to ensure your keywords remain relevant and effective.

Creating Compelling Meta Tags And Descriptions

Creating compelling meta tags and descriptions is an essential part of optimizing your website for search engines and attracting clicks from users. Here are some tips for crafting effective meta tags and descriptions:

Meta Title: The meta title appears as the clickable headline in search engine results. It should be concise, relevant, and include your target keyword. Aim for a length of around 50-60 characters to ensure it doesn't get cut off in search results.

Meta Description: The meta description provides a brief summary of the page's content. It should be persuasive, engaging, and accurately describe what users can expect when they click on your page. Include your target keyword naturally and aim for a length of around 150-160 characters.

Unique and Descriptive: Each page on your website should have a unique meta title and description that accurately reflects the content of that specific page. Avoid duplicating meta tags across multiple pages, as this can confuse search engines and users.

Use Actionable Language: Use action-oriented language to encourage users to click on your listing. Include words like "discover," "learn," "find," "explore," or "get" to evoke curiosity and entice users to visit your website.

Highlight Unique Selling Points: If applicable, highlight any unique selling points or key features of your content or products/services in your meta description. This can help differentiate your listing from competitors and attract more relevant clicks.

Be Clear and Concise: Make sure your meta tags and descriptions are clear, concise, and easy to understand. Avoid using jargon or technical terms that may confuse users. Use plain language that appeals to your target audience.

Test and Optimize: Monitor the performance of your meta tags and descriptions using analytics tools. Test different variations to see which ones generate more clicks and adjust accordingly. Continuously optimize and refine your meta tags to improve your click-through rates.

Stay Within Character Limits: Search engines have character limits for meta titles and descriptions. Make sure your tags fit within those limits to ensure they are fully displayed in search results.

Remember, meta tags and descriptions are not direct ranking factors for search engines, but they play a crucial role in attracting clicks and influencing user behavior. By crafting compelling and relevant meta tags and descriptions, you can improve your website's visibility, click-through rates, and overall SEO performance.

Optimizing Headings, Subheadings, And Content Structure

Optimizing headings, subheadings, and content structure is an important aspect of on-page SEO. Here are some techniques to help you optimize these elements:

Use H1 Tags for Main Headings: The H1 tag should be used for the main heading of your page or article. It should accurately summarize the main topic or focus of the content. Including your target keyword in the H1 tag can help search engines understand the relevance of your content.

Utilize H2-H6 Tags for Subheadings: Use H2-H6 tags to organize your content into logical sections. These subheadings provide structure and hierarchy to your content, making it easier for readers and search engines to navigate and understand the information. Include relevant keywords in your subheadings to further optimize your content.

Keep Headings Descriptive and Clear: Your headings should accurately describe the content that follows. Clear and descriptive headings help both users and search engines understand the context and relevance of your content. Avoid using generic or vague headings that don't provide meaningful information.

Maintain Consistency in Heading Structure: Consistency in heading structure improves the readability and user experience of your content. Use a consistent hierarchy of headings throughout your page or article. For example, use H2 tags for main sections, H3 tags for sub-sections, and so on. This helps users easily scan and navigate your content.

Use Keywords Naturally: Incorporate relevant keywords into your headings and subheadings, but do so naturally. Avoid keyword stuffing or over-optimization, as this can negatively impact the user experience and search engine rankings. Focus on creating informative and engaging headings that accurately represent the content.

Break Content into Digestible Sections: Break your content into smaller, easily digestible sections using subheadings. This improves readability and makes it easier for users to find the specific information they're looking for. Use descriptive subheadings that accurately summarize the content within each section.

Use Bullet Points and Numbered Lists: When appropriate, use bullet points and numbered lists to present information in a concise and organized manner. This helps readers quickly grasp key points and enhances the readability of your content. It also makes your content more scannable for users who prefer to skim.

Incorporate Relevant Multimedia Elements: Enhance your content by including relevant multimedia elements such as images, videos, infographics, or charts. These elements can help break up text and make your content more visually appealing and engaging. Optimize multimedia elements by providing descriptive alt text and captions, and compress images for faster loading times.

By optimizing headings, subheadings, and content structure, you can improve the user experience, make your content more appealing to readers, and signal to search engines the relevance and organization of your information. Remember to focus on providing valuable and informative content that satisfies user intent while incorporating relevant keywords naturally throughout your headings and content.

Best Practices For Url Structure And Internal Linking

URL structure and internal linking are crucial for SEO and user experience. Here are some best practices to follow:

URL Structure:

- Keep URLs Descriptive: Ensure that your URLs are descriptive and provide an indication of what the page is about. Use keywords related to the content of the page and avoid generic or random strings of characters.
- Use Hyphens as Separators: Use hyphens (-) to separate words in your URL. Hyphens are preferred by search engines and make URLs more readable for both users and search engines.
- Keep URLs Short and Simple: Shorter URLs are easier to remember and share. Aim for concise URLs that accurately represent the content of the page. Avoid using unnecessary words, numbers, or parameters in your URLs.
- Avoid Dynamic URLs: Dynamic URLs with long query strings or parameters can be challenging for search engines to crawl and index. Whenever possible, use static URLs that are more search engine and user-friendly.

Internal Linking:

- Use Descriptive Anchor Text: When creating internal links, use descriptive and relevant anchor text that accurately describes the destination page. Avoid generic terms like "click here" or "read more." Descriptive anchor text helps search engines understand the context and relevance of the linked page.
- Link to Relevant and Related Content: Link to other pages on your website that are relevant and related

to the current page's topic. This helps search engines understand the content structure of your website and improves user navigation.

- Create a Logical Link Structure: Establish a logical link structure within your website. Make sure important pages are easily accessible through the navigation menu or internal links. Create a hierarchy of pages, with the most important or high-traffic pages having more internal links pointing to them.

- Avoid Excessive Internal Linking: While internal linking is important, avoid excessive linking that may confuse or overwhelm users. Only include relevant and useful internal links that add value to the content.

- Use Sitemaps: Create an XML sitemap and submit it to search engines. A sitemap helps search engines discover and understand the structure of your website, including internal links.

- Monitor Broken Links: Regularly check for broken links within your website and fix them promptly. Broken links can negatively impact user experience and hinder search engine crawling.

- Consider User Flow and Behavior: When implementing internal links, consider the user flow and behavior on your website. Guide users to related and relevant content that enhances their overall experience and encourages them to explore further.

By following these best practices for URL structure and internal linking, you can improve the visibility and accessibility of your website for both search engines and users. Clear and descriptive URLs make it easier for search engines to understand the content, while strategic internal linking enhances navigation and helps search engines establish the relevance and hierarchy of your pages.

Mobile Optimization And Page Speed Considerations

Mobile optimization and page speed are crucial factors for SEO and user experience. Here are some best practices to consider:

Mobile Optimization:

- Responsive Design: Ensure that your website is mobile-friendly and responsive. Responsive design automatically adjusts the layout and elements of your website to fit different screen sizes and devices. This provides a seamless experience for mobile users.
- Mobile-Friendly Test: Use Google's Mobile-Friendly Test or other similar tools to check if your website is optimized for mobile devices. These tests analyze your website and provide recommendations to improve mobile compatibility.
- User-Friendly Mobile Navigation: Design your mobile navigation in a way that is easy to use and navigate on smaller screens. Utilize drop-down menus, collapsible sections, or a hamburger menu to save space and enhance user experience.
- Optimize Content for Mobile Reading: Ensure that your content is easily readable on mobile devices. Use legible font sizes, proper line spacing, and clear headings to improve readability. Avoid large blocks of text and consider breaking content into smaller paragraphs.
- Mobile-Specific SEO Considerations: Pay attention to mobile-specific SEO elements, such as mobile-friendly tags and mobile XML sitemaps. These elements help search engines understand that your website is optimized for mobile users.

Page Speed Considerations:

- Optimize Image Sizes: Compress and optimize images

to reduce their file sizes without compromising quality. Large images can significantly slow down page loading times. Use image compression tools or plugins to optimize your images.

- Enable Browser Caching: Leverage browser caching by setting cache expiration headers on your server. This allows returning visitors to load your web pages faster by storing certain resources in their browser cache.
- Minify CSS, JavaScript, and HTML: Minify your website's CSS, JavaScript, and HTML files by removing unnecessary characters, white spaces, and comments. This reduces file sizes and improves page loading speed.
- Enable GZIP Compression: Enable GZIP compression on your server to reduce the file size of your website's resources before they are sent to the user's browser. GZIP compression significantly reduces the time it takes to transfer data.
- Reduce Redirects: Minimize the number of redirects on your website as each redirect adds an extra HTTP request, which can slow down page loading time. Ensure that your website uses proper redirect practices, such as using 301 redirects for permanent URL changes.
- Content Delivery Network (CDN): Consider using a CDN to deliver your website's content from servers located closer to the user's geographical location. This reduces the physical distance between the user and your server, improving page load times.
- Regular Performance Monitoring: Monitor your website's performance using tools like Google PageSpeed Insights or GTmetrix. These tools provide insights and recommendations for improving page speed.

By implementing mobile optimization techniques and optimizing your website for fast page loading, you enhance the user experience and increase the chances of better search engine rankings. Mobile-friendly websites and fast-loading pages are more likely to rank higher in mobile search results and provide a positive experience for visitors accessing your website on mobile devices.

VI. User Experience and Engagement Signals

Importance Of User Experience In Evergreen Algorithms

User experience plays a vital role in the success of evergreen algorithms. Evergreen algorithms, such as Google's Panda, Penguin, Hummingbird, RankBrain, and BERT, are designed to provide users with the most relevant and valuable search results based on their queries. These algorithms aim to deliver a positive user experience by ensuring that the search results are high-quality, relevant, and satisfy user intent.

Here's why user experience is essential in evergreen algorithms:

User Satisfaction: Evergreen algorithms prioritize user satisfaction by focusing on delivering search results that meet the user's needs. If a website provides a positive user experience with valuable content, easy navigation, and a pleasing design, it is more likely to rank higher in search results.

Engagement Metrics: Evergreen algorithms consider various engagement metrics, such as click-through rates (CTR), bounce rates, time on page, and dwell time. These metrics indicate how users interact with a website and whether they find the content helpful and engaging. Websites with better user experiences tend to have higher engagement metrics, which positively impact their rankings.

Content Quality: User experience and content quality go hand in hand. Evergreen algorithms emphasize delivering high-quality, relevant content to users. Websites that prioritize user experience tend to create valuable, informative, and well-structured content that satisfies user intent. This, in turn, improves their chances of ranking well in search results.

Mobile-Friendliness: With the increasing number of users accessing the internet through mobile devices, evergreen algorithms give importance to mobile-friendliness. Websites that offer a responsive design, mobile-friendly navigation, and fast-loading pages provide a better user experience on mobile devices, leading to improved rankings.

User Feedback: Evergreen algorithms consider user feedback and signals to refine search results. Positive user reviews, social media mentions, and other user-generated signals indicate that a website provides a positive user experience. These signals can influence the ranking of a website in search results.

Return Visitors: Websites that offer a great user experience are more likely to have repeat visitors. Evergreen algorithms consider the number of return visitors as an indicator of user satisfaction and relevance. Websites that consistently provide a positive experience tend to have higher user loyalty and improved search rankings.

By focusing on user experience, website owners can align their efforts with evergreen algorithms and improve their visibility in search results. Providing valuable, user-friendly content, optimizing website performance, ensuring mobile-friendliness, and prioritizing engagement metrics are key steps to enhance the user experience and gain visibility in the ever-evolving digital landscape.

Enhancing Website Design And Navigation

Enhancing website design and navigation is crucial for providing a positive user experience and improving your website's performance in search engine rankings. Here are some key strategies to consider:

Responsive Design: Ensure that your website is designed to be responsive, meaning it adapts to different screen sizes and devices. This is particularly important in the mobile-first era, as more users access the internet through smartphones and tablets. A responsive design ensures that your website looks and functions well on all devices, providing a seamless experience for users.

Intuitive Navigation: Simplify your website's navigation structure to make it easy for users to find what they're looking for. Use clear and descriptive menu labels, organize content into logical categories, and include a search function to assist users in finding specific information. Avoid clutter and excessive dropdown menus, as they can confuse and overwhelm visitors.

User-Friendly Layout: Optimize your website layout for readability and ease of use. Use legible fonts, appropriate font sizes, and sufficient white space to improve readability. Consider the F-pattern or Z-pattern layout for arranging important content elements, as they align with users' natural reading patterns. Place important information and calls to action prominently on the page to guide users.

Fast Loading Speed: Page load speed is a critical factor for user experience and SEO. Optimize your website's performance by minimizing file sizes, compressing images, enabling browser caching, and using content delivery networks (CDNs) to serve your website's assets from servers closer to the user's location. A fast-loading website keeps users engaged and reduces bounce rates.

Consistent Branding: Maintain a consistent visual identity throughout your website, including color schemes, typography, and brand elements. Consistency helps users identify and connect with your brand, enhancing their overall experience. Ensure that your logo is prominently displayed and use visual cues, such as icons or buttons, to guide users through the website.

Clear Calls to Action (CTAs): Incorporate clear and compelling CTAs throughout your website to guide users towards desired actions, such as making a purchase, signing up for a newsletter, or contacting you. Use visually distinct buttons or links, accompanied by persuasive copy, to encourage user engagement.

User Testing and Feedback: Regularly conduct user testing and gather feedback to identify areas for improvement. Observing how users navigate your website, understanding their pain points, and incorporating their suggestions can help refine the design and navigation to better meet their needs.

Remember, a well-designed and user-friendly website not only improves the overall user experience but also encourages visitors to stay longer, explore more content, and take desired actions. By enhancing website design and navigation, you create a positive impression on users, increase engagement, and improve your website's chances of ranking higher in search engine results.

Improving Page Load Speed And Mobile Responsiveness

Improving page load speed and mobile responsiveness are crucial factors for enhancing user experience and SEO. Here are some techniques to optimize these aspects:

Image Optimization: Compress images without sacrificing quality to reduce file size. Use image formats like JPEG or WebP and utilize tools to optimize images automatically. Additionally, specify image dimensions in HTML to prevent layout shifts and improve load times.

Minify CSS, JavaScript, and HTML: Remove unnecessary characters, spaces, and line breaks from code files to reduce their size. This can be done manually or through automated tools. Smaller file sizes result in faster load times.

Enable Browser Caching: Set up caching directives on your server to instruct the user's browser to store certain files, such as CSS and JavaScript, locally. This allows returning visitors to load your site faster since they don't need to retrieve those files again.

Content Delivery Network (CDN): Use a CDN to distribute your website's static content across multiple servers located in different geographical regions. This helps deliver content more quickly to users, especially those located far from your server's location.

Responsive Design: Ensure your website is mobile-friendly and adapts to different screen sizes and devices. Use responsive design techniques to automatically adjust content and layout based on the user's device, providing an optimal viewing experience.

AMP (Accelerated Mobile Pages): Consider implementing Accelerated Mobile Pages (AMP), a framework that focuses on fast-loading mobile web pages. AMP optimizes page performance and improves mobile responsiveness, enhancing the user experience on mobile devices.

Reduce Redirects: Minimize the use of redirects as they add extra time to the page load process. Ensure that any redirects are necessary and point to the most appropriate destination.

Prioritize Above-the-Fold Content: Load the most critical elements of your webpage first, such as headline, main content, and primary call-to-action. This gives users a sense of fast loading and allows them to start engaging with the page while other elements continue to load.

Test and Monitor Performance: Regularly test your website's performance using tools like Google PageSpeed Insights, GTmetrix, or Pingdom. Monitor load times, server response times, and other performance metrics to identify areas for improvement and track progress over time.

By implementing these strategies, you can significantly improve the page load speed and mobile responsiveness of your website. This not only enhances the user experience but also boosts your website's visibility in search engine rankings, as search engines prioritize fast and mobile-friendly websites.

Optimizing For User Engagement And Reducing Bounce Rate

Optimizing for user engagement and reducing bounce rate is crucial for improving the overall performance and success of your website. Here are some strategies to achieve this:

Create Compelling and Relevant Content: Ensure that your content is informative, valuable, and relevant to your target audience. Use engaging language, provide actionable insights, and make your content visually appealing with images, videos, and infographics.

Improve Readability: Use clear and concise writing style, break up content into shorter paragraphs, and utilize headings, subheadings, and bullet points to make it easy to scan and digest. Incorporate white space and proper formatting to enhance readability.

Implement Clear Call-to-Actions (CTAs): Guide your visitors towards the desired actions by placing clear and prominent CTAs throughout your website. Make them visually appealing and use persuasive language to encourage engagement, such as "Learn More," "Sign Up," or "Buy Now."

Enhance Website Navigation: Ensure that your website is easy to navigate with a clear menu structure and logical hierarchy. Use descriptive labels for menu items and include a search function to help users find what they're looking for quickly.

Optimize Page Load Speed: Slow-loading pages can lead to high bounce rates. Compress images, minify CSS and JavaScript files, and leverage browser caching to improve page load speed. Monitor and optimize server response times to ensure fast and efficient delivery of your webpages.

Mobile-Friendly Design: With the majority of internet users accessing websites from mobile devices, it's crucial to have a responsive design that provides a seamless experience across different screen sizes. Optimize your website for mobile by using mobile-friendly layouts, readable fonts, and touch-friendly elements.

Engage with Interactive Elements: Incorporate interactive elements such as quizzes, polls, surveys, and comment sections to encourage user participation and extend their time on your website. These elements can foster a sense of community and increase engagement.

Personalize User Experience: Utilize personalization techniques to deliver customized content and recommendations based on user preferences, browsing history, or location. This can enhance user engagement by providing a more tailored and relevant experience.

Improve Page Loading Experience: Use lazy loading techniques to load content as the user scrolls down the page, reducing initial load times. Additionally, avoid intrusive pop-ups or interstitials that may disrupt the user's browsing experience.

Analyze and Optimize: Regularly analyze user behavior and engagement metrics using tools like Google Analytics. Identify pages with high bounce rates and low engagement and make data-driven optimizations to improve their performance.

By implementing these strategies, you can optimize your website for user engagement and reduce bounce rates. Engaged visitors are more likely to stay on your site, explore more pages, and take desired actions, leading to improved conversions and overall success for your online presence.

Leveraging Social Signals And User-Generated Content

Leveraging social signals and user-generated content can significantly impact user engagement and SEO. Here are some strategies to make the most of these elements:

Encourage Social Sharing: Make it easy for visitors to share your content by including social sharing buttons on your website. This allows users to share your content with their social networks, increasing its visibility and potential reach. Additionally, regularly post your content on social media platforms and actively engage with your audience to foster a community and encourage social sharing.

Engage with User-Generated Content: User-generated content, such as reviews, testimonials, and comments, adds credibility and authenticity to your website. Encourage users to leave reviews or provide feedback on your products or services. Display user-generated content prominently on your website, as it can influence the purchasing decisions of other visitors.

Foster Social Proof: Showcase social proof, such as the number of followers, likes, shares, or positive testimonials, to build trust and credibility with your audience. Display social proof prominently on your website to demonstrate that others value and trust your brand.

Encourage User Interaction: Implement features that encourage user interaction, such as comments sections, forums, or discussion boards. This not only enhances user engagement but also provides valuable user-generated content that can drive organic traffic and improve search engine rankings.

Run Contests or Giveaways: Engage your audience by running contests or giveaways on social media platforms. Encourage users to participate by liking, sharing, or commenting on your content. This generates social signals and increases brand visibility.

Monitor and Respond to Social Mentions: Regularly monitor social media platforms for mentions of your brand or content. Respond to user comments, questions, and feedback promptly. Engaging with your audience demonstrates that you value their input and helps build a positive brand reputation.

Embed Social Media Feeds: Embedding social media feeds on your website can showcase real-time updates and social interactions. It encourages users to follow and engage with your brand on social media platforms.

Utilize Social Media Advertising: Social media advertising allows you to reach a broader audience and target specific demographics. Running targeted ads can drive traffic to your website, increase engagement, and potentially generate more user-generated content.

Remember to always adhere to best practices and guidelines for social media usage and user-generated content. Encourage genuine interactions and provide a positive user experience to foster engagement and build a strong online presence.

VII. Monitoring, Analyzing, and Adapting

Utilizing Seo Analytics Tools To Track Performance

Utilizing SEO analytics tools is crucial for tracking the performance of your website and SEO efforts. These tools provide valuable insights into various metrics and data points that help you understand how your website is performing and identify areas for improvement. Here are some popular SEO analytics tools to consider:

Google Analytics: Google Analytics is a free tool that provides comprehensive website analytics. It offers a wealth of data, including traffic sources, user behavior, conversion rates, and more. You can track key metrics like organic traffic, bounce rate, average session duration, and goal completions. It also integrates with other Google tools like Search Console, allowing you to access additional SEO data.

Google Search Console: Google Search Console is another free tool from Google that focuses specifically on your website's performance in search results. It provides data on keywords, impressions, click-through rates, and average position in search results. It also alerts you to any indexing or crawling issues that may affect your website's visibility.

Moz: Moz offers a suite of SEO tools that can help you monitor and improve your website's performance. Their tools provide insights into keyword rankings, backlink profiles, on-page optimization, and site audits. Moz also offers a unique metric called Domain Authority, which measures the overall authority and credibility of a website.

SEMrush: SEMrush is a powerful SEO tool that offers a wide range of features for keyword research, competitor analysis, site audits, and more. It provides detailed data on organic search traffic, backlinks, and keyword rankings. SEMrush also offers competitive analysis tools to help you identify opportunities and stay ahead of your competitors.

Ahrefs: Ahrefs is a comprehensive SEO toolset that includes features like keyword research, backlink analysis, content explorer, and rank tracking. It provides detailed insights into your website's backlink profile, allowing you to monitor the quality and quantity of your backlinks. Ahrefs also offers competitor analysis tools to help you identify their top-performing content and backlink sources.

Yoast SEO: If you're using WordPress for your website, the Yoast SEO plugin is a valuable tool. It provides on-page optimization guidance, analyzes your content for SEO best practices, and helps you create search engine-friendly meta tags and descriptions. Yoast SEO also offers readability analysis to ensure your content is engaging and easy to read.

When using SEO analytics tools, it's important to regularly review and analyze the data to make informed decisions and optimize your SEO strategies. Track important metrics like organic traffic, keyword rankings, conversion rates, and user engagement to gauge the effectiveness of your SEO efforts and identify areas for improvement.

Monitoring Search Engine Rankings And Organic Traffic

Monitoring search engine rankings and organic traffic is an essential part of SEO. By tracking your website's rankings and traffic, you can evaluate the effectiveness of your SEO strategies and identify opportunities for improvement. Here are some key aspects to consider when monitoring search engine rankings and organic traffic:

Keyword Rankings: Use tools like Google Search Console, SEMrush, or Ahrefs to track your website's keyword rankings. Monitor how your targeted keywords are performing over time and identify any fluctuations or changes. This allows you to assess the impact of your optimization efforts and make adjustments as needed.

Organic Traffic: Analyze your website's organic traffic using tools like Google Analytics. Keep an eye on the overall organic traffic trends, including the number of visitors, sessions, and pageviews coming from organic search. Compare the data over time to identify any significant increases or decreases, and correlate them with your SEO activities.

Landing Pages: Examine which pages on your website are driving the most organic traffic. Identify the pages that are performing well and those that may need improvement. Assess the relevance and quality of the content on these pages and consider optimizing them further to capitalize on their success.

Conversion Rates: Look at the conversion rates of your organic traffic. Are visitors taking the desired actions on your website, such as making a purchase, submitting a form, or signing up for a newsletter? By analyzing conversion rates, you can understand the effectiveness of your website in converting organic traffic into valuable outcomes.

Traffic Sources: Explore the sources of your organic traffic. Are there any specific search engines, regions, or devices that are driving the majority of your organic traffic? Understanding these patterns can help you tailor your SEO strategies and optimize your website for specific target audiences.

Competitor Analysis: Monitor the organic rankings and traffic of your competitors. Identify their top-performing pages and keywords and compare them to your own. This analysis can provide insights into potential gaps in your SEO strategy and help you identify opportunities for improvement.

Regular Reporting: Create regular reports to track and analyze the key metrics related to search engine rankings and organic traffic. This allows you to monitor progress, identify trends, and make data-driven decisions to optimize your SEO efforts.

Remember, search engine rankings and organic traffic can fluctuate, so it's important to monitor them over time and assess the overall trends. By staying vigilant and responsive to changes, you can adapt your SEO strategies to maintain and improve your website's visibility and organic traffic.

Analyzing User Behavior And Engagement Metrics

Analyzing user behavior and engagement metrics is crucial for understanding how visitors interact with your website and optimizing it for better user experience. Here are some key metrics and methods for analyzing user behavior and engagement:

Bounce Rate: Bounce rate indicates the percentage of visitors who leave your website without interacting with any other pages. A high bounce rate may suggest that visitors are not finding what they are looking for or that your website's content or design needs improvement.

Time on Page: This metric measures the average amount of time visitors spend on a specific page. It can indicate the level of engagement and interest in your content. Longer average time on page often suggests that visitors are finding value in your content.

Page Views: Page views refer to the number of times a particular page has been viewed by visitors. Tracking page views helps you identify popular content and areas of interest on your website.

Click-through Rate (CTR): CTR measures the percentage of users who click on a specific link or call-to-action. It is commonly used to analyze the effectiveness of your website's elements, such as headlines, meta descriptions, and call-to-action buttons.

Conversion Rate: Conversion rate measures the percentage of visitors who take a desired action on your website, such as making a purchase, filling out a form, or subscribing to a newsletter. Analyzing conversion rates helps you evaluate the effectiveness of your website in achieving its goals.

Heatmaps and Scrollmaps: Heatmaps provide visual representations of where users click or interact the most on your website, while scrollmaps show how far users scroll down a page. These tools help you understand user behavior patterns and optimize your website's layout and content placement.

Exit Pages: Exit pages show the pages where visitors leave your website. Analyzing exit pages can reveal potential issues or gaps in your content that may be causing visitors to leave without converting.

User Feedback: Collecting user feedback through surveys, feedback forms, or user testing sessions can provide valuable insights into user preferences, pain points, and areas of improvement.

By analyzing these user behavior and engagement metrics, you can identify strengths and weaknesses in your website's design, content, and user experience. This information can guide you in making data-driven decisions to optimize your website, improve engagement, and increase conversions.

Identifying Algorithmic Changes And Adapting Strategies

Identifying algorithmic changes in search engines, particularly in major search engines like Google, is crucial for staying ahead in SEO. Here are some strategies to help you identify algorithmic changes and adapt your SEO strategies accordingly:

Stay Informed: Keep yourself updated with industry news, SEO blogs, forums, and official announcements from search engines. Follow reputable sources that provide insights and analysis on algorithmic changes and updates. This will help you stay informed about the latest developments in the SEO landscape.

Monitor Rankings and Traffic: Regularly monitor your website's rankings and organic traffic. Sudden drops or fluctuations in rankings and traffic can indicate potential algorithmic changes. Use SEO analytics tools and rank tracking software to keep a close eye on your website's performance.

Google Search Console: Utilize Google Search Console, a free tool provided by Google, to monitor your website's performance in search results. It provides valuable information about indexing, search queries, and any issues that may affect your website's visibility.

Algorithm Watchdogs: Some SEO tools and websites specialize in tracking and reporting algorithmic changes. They analyze search results and provide insights into potential updates. Examples include Mozcast, SEMrush Sensor, and Algoroo.

Analyze Industry Trends: Keep an eye on trends and patterns within your industry. Algorithmic changes often target specific industries or types of websites. By understanding industry trends and observing how competitors are affected, you can gain insights into potential algorithmic shifts.

Google's Official Guidelines: Familiarize yourself with Google's

Webmaster Guidelines. These guidelines provide valuable information about best practices for website optimization and SEO. Staying aligned with Google's guidelines helps you adapt your strategies to any algorithmic changes that prioritize certain ranking factors.

Test and Experiment: Continuously test and experiment with your SEO strategies. Implement changes and monitor their impact on your website's performance. By testing different approaches and closely analyzing the results, you can adapt to algorithmic changes and refine your SEO strategies.

Diversify Your SEO Efforts: Avoid relying solely on one SEO strategy or tactic. Diversify your optimization efforts by focusing on various aspects of SEO, such as content quality, backlink profile, user experience, and technical optimization. This helps you build a strong foundation that can withstand algorithmic changes.

Remember that search engine algorithms are dynamic, and they evolve to provide the best user experience and relevant search results. By staying informed, monitoring performance, and adapting your strategies, you can navigate algorithmic changes effectively and maintain a strong presence in search engine rankings.

Continuous Testing And Optimization For Long-Term Success

Continuous testing and optimization are crucial for achieving long-term success in SEO. The digital landscape is constantly evolving, and search engine algorithms are continuously refined to deliver the best user experience and relevant search results. To stay competitive and maintain a strong online presence, here are some strategies for continuous testing and optimization:

A/B Testing: Conduct A/B tests to compare different variations of your web pages, such as headlines, calls-to-action, layouts, or content formats. Test one element at a time and measure the impact on user engagement, conversions, and search engine rankings. Use tools like Google Optimize or Optimizely to set up and analyze A/B tests.

Conversion Rate Optimization (CRO): Focus on optimizing your website for conversions. Analyze user behavior using tools like Google Analytics to identify areas of improvement. Test different page elements, such as forms, buttons, colors, and content placement, to optimize your conversion funnel and improve your website's performance.

Content Updates: Regularly review and update your content to ensure it remains relevant and valuable to your audience. Conduct keyword research to identify new opportunities and trends, and optimize your content accordingly. Refreshing and expanding existing content can also help improve its visibility and rankings in search results.

Technical SEO Audits: Perform regular technical SEO audits to identify and fix any issues that may impact your website's performance and visibility. Check for broken links, crawl errors, duplicate content, and page load speed issues. Use tools like Screaming Frog or SEMrush to conduct comprehensive audits and make necessary optimizations.

User Experience (UX) Optimization: Continuously improve the user experience of your website. Pay attention to factors such as site navigation, mobile-friendliness, page speed, and intuitive design. Conduct usability tests, gather user feedback, and make data-driven improvements to enhance the overall user experience.

Backlink Profile Analysis: Monitor and analyze your backlink profile to ensure it remains healthy and authoritative. Disavow any low-quality or spammy links that could negatively impact your website's rankings. Build high-quality backlinks through outreach, content promotion, and relationship building with industry influencers and authoritative websites.

Mobile Optimization: As mobile usage continues to grow, prioritize mobile optimization. Ensure your website is fully responsive, loads quickly on mobile devices, and provides a seamless user experience across different screen sizes. Optimize your content for mobile search intent and implement mobile-specific SEO techniques.

Stay Updated with Industry Trends: Continuously educate yourself about the latest SEO trends, algorithm updates, and best practices. Follow reputable industry blogs, attend conferences, participate in forums, and engage with SEO communities. Staying updated with industry trends helps you adapt your strategies and stay ahead of the competition.

Remember, SEO is an ongoing process, and it requires a commitment to continuous improvement and adaptation. By testing and optimizing your website, content, user experience, and backlink profile, you can enhance your online visibility, attract more organic traffic, and achieve long-term success in SEO.

VIII. Future Trends and Evolving Evergreen Algorithms

Emerging Technologies And Their Impact On Algorithms

Emerging technologies have a significant impact on search engine algorithms, as they continuously evolve to provide more relevant and personalized search results. Here are some emerging technologies and their influence on search engine algorithms:

Artificial Intelligence (AI) and Machine Learning: AI and machine learning technologies have transformed search engines' ability to understand user queries and deliver more accurate results. Algorithms powered by AI can analyze vast amounts of data, learn from user behavior, and improve search results based on user intent and context. Google's RankBrain and BERT are examples of AI-driven algorithms that enhance search relevance and understanding.

Natural Language Processing (NLP): NLP enables search engines to understand and interpret human language, including conversational queries and voice search. Algorithms are becoming more adept at understanding the intent behind user queries and providing more relevant results based on the context of the search.

Voice Search and Virtual Assistants: The rise of voice search and virtual assistants, like Amazon Alexa, Google Assistant, and Apple Siri, has led to advancements in search algorithms. Voice search algorithms focus on delivering concise, conversational answers to user queries, as voice searches often have a more conversational and natural language structure.

Mobile and Responsive Design: With the increasing dominance of mobile devices, search engines have placed a strong emphasis on mobile-friendliness and responsive design. Algorithms prioritize websites that provide a seamless mobile user experience, including fast load times, mobile-friendly layouts, and easy navigation on smaller screens.

Local Search and Geolocation: Algorithms have evolved to better serve localized search results. Location-based technologies, such as GPS and geolocation data, enable search engines to deliver location-specific results and personalized recommendations for businesses, services, and attractions in the user's vicinity.

Visual Search: Visual search technology allows users to search for information using images rather than text-based queries. Search engines use visual recognition algorithms to analyze images and provide relevant results. This technology is particularly relevant for e-commerce, fashion, and visually-oriented industries.

User Behavior Analysis: Algorithms now consider user behavior signals, such as click-through rates (CTR), bounce rates, and dwell time, to determine the relevance and quality of search results. Analyzing user behavior helps search engines refine their algorithms and deliver more valuable and engaging content to users.

It's important for website owners and SEO practitioners to stay updated on emerging technologies and their impact on search algorithms. By understanding these trends, you can adapt your SEO strategies to align with the evolving search landscape and leverage emerging technologies to improve your website's visibility and performance in search engine results pages.

Voice Search And Natural Language Processing Advancements

Voice search and natural language processing (NLP) advancements have revolutionized the way people interact with search engines and have had a significant impact on search algorithms. Here's a closer look at voice search and NLP and how they have advanced in recent years:

Voice Search: Voice search allows users to perform searches by speaking their queries instead of typing them. With the widespread adoption of voice-activated devices like smartphones, smart speakers, and virtual assistants, voice search has become increasingly popular. Advancements in speech recognition technology have greatly improved the accuracy of voice recognition, making it easier for search engines to understand and process spoken queries.

Natural Language Processing (NLP): NLP is a branch of artificial intelligence that focuses on the interaction between computers and human language. It enables search engines to understand and interpret natural language queries, including complex sentence structures, conversational language, and context. NLP algorithms analyze the semantics, intent, and meaning behind user queries to provide more relevant search results.

Conversational Search: With voice search, users tend to use more conversational and natural language when asking questions. Search engines have adapted to this shift by developing conversational search capabilities. Instead of relying on keyword matching, algorithms now aim to understand the intent and context of the entire query to deliver more precise results.

Featured Snippets and Direct Answers: Voice search has led to the rise of featured snippets and direct answers, which are concise, voice-friendly responses that directly address the user's query. Search engines extract information from web pages and present it prominently in search results, making it easily accessible to voice search users.

Contextual Understanding: NLP advancements enable search engines to better understand the context of a query by considering factors such as the user's location, search history, and device. This allows for more personalized and relevant search results tailored to the individual user.

Multilingual Voice Search: Voice search technology has expanded to support multiple languages, making it accessible to a global audience. Search engines have made significant progress in understanding and processing different languages, dialects, and accents, enabling users worldwide to benefit from voice search capabilities.

- To optimize for voice search and NLP advancements, consider the following strategies:
- Focus on conversational keywords and long-tail phrases that reflect how people naturally speak.
- Provide direct, concise answers to commonly asked questions related to your industry or niche.
- Optimize your website content to be mobile-friendly and easily scannable for voice-based results.
- Include structured data markup on your web pages to provide additional context and information to search engines.
- Improve your website's loading speed to accommodate voice search users who expect quick responses.
- Monitor and analyze voice search data to identify trends and opportunities for optimizing your content and user experience.

By understanding the advancements in voice search and NLP, you can adapt your SEO strategies to cater to the growing number of users who rely on voice-activated devices and natural language queries. Embracing these advancements will help you stay ahead of the curve and provide a seamless search experience for your audience.

Mobile-First Indexing And Mobile User Experience Considerations

Mobile-first indexing is an approach that search engines, particularly Google, have adopted to prioritize the mobile version of websites when determining search rankings. With the increasing use of mobile devices for browsing the internet, optimizing for mobile has become essential for SEO success. Here are some key considerations for mobile-first indexing and mobile user experience:

Responsive Design: Ensure your website is built with a responsive design that adapts to different screen sizes and resolutions. This allows your content to be displayed properly on various devices, including smartphones and tablets.

Mobile-Friendly Layout: Design your mobile website with a user-friendly layout that is easy to navigate on smaller screens. Use clear and concise menus, intuitive navigation, and properly sized buttons for better user experience.

Page Loading Speed: Mobile users expect fast-loading pages, so optimize your website's speed by minimizing file sizes, leveraging browser caching, and reducing unnecessary code or scripts. Mobile users are often on the go and have limited data plans, so faster loading times can significantly improve their experience.

Visual and Content Optimization: Optimize your visuals, such as images and videos, for mobile devices by compressing them without compromising quality. Use legible fonts and appropriate font sizes to ensure easy reading on smaller screens. Break up content into shorter paragraphs and use headings and bullet points to improve readability.

Mobile-Specific SEO: Consider mobile-specific SEO strategies, such as optimizing for local search, as mobile searches often have a strong local intent. Utilize mobile-friendly structured data markup to enhance search engine understanding of your mobile content.

Mobile Usability Testing: Test your website's mobile usability across different devices and screen sizes to ensure a smooth experience. Pay attention to touch elements' responsiveness, form entry, and overall functionality. Address any issues or errors that may arise during testing.

Mobile-Optimized Calls to Action: Make sure your calls to action (CTAs) are easily clickable and prominent on mobile devices. Users should be able to complete desired actions, such as filling out forms or making purchases, with minimal effort.

Mobile Analytics and Tracking: Set up mobile-specific analytics to track mobile user behavior, engagement, and conversions. Gain insights into mobile-specific metrics and identify areas for improvement in the mobile user experience.

Mobile App Optimization: If you have a mobile app, optimize it for search engines and ensure a seamless transition between your mobile website and app. Implement app indexing and deep linking strategies to increase app visibility in search results.

Continuous Optimization: Regularly monitor and optimize your mobile site based on user feedback, analytics data, and emerging mobile trends. Stay up to date with mobile SEO best practices and algorithm changes to maintain a competitive edge.

By prioritizing mobile-first indexing and optimizing the mobile user experience, you can enhance your website's visibility, engagement, and conversions on mobile devices. Embracing a mobile-first approach is essential for staying relevant in the ever-growing mobile landscape and providing a positive user experience for your mobile audience.

The Rise Of Artificial Intelligence In Search Algorithms

The rise of artificial intelligence (AI) has had a significant impact on search algorithms, revolutionizing the way search engines understand and deliver search results. AI-powered algorithms, such as Google's RankBrain and BERT, have brought about advancements in natural language processing and semantic understanding, enabling search engines to provide more relevant and contextually accurate search results. Here are some key aspects to consider regarding the role of AI in search algorithms:

Machine Learning: AI-powered search algorithms utilize machine learning techniques to analyze vast amounts of data and learn patterns and trends. This allows search engines to continuously improve their understanding of user intent and deliver more relevant search results.

Natural Language Processing (NLP): NLP enables search engines to better understand and interpret the meaning behind search queries. AI algorithms can now process complex language structures, decipher user intent, and provide more accurate search results based on contextual understanding.

Semantic Search: AI has enabled search engines to move beyond keyword-based matching and focus on semantic search, which aims to understand the meaning and context of words and phrases. By analyzing the relationships between words and entities, search algorithms can deliver more precise and contextually relevant results.

User Intent Recognition: AI algorithms excel in recognizing user intent behind search queries. They can identify whether a user is seeking information, looking to make a purchase, or searching for specific content. This allows search engines to provide more targeted results that align with the user's intent.

Personalization: AI-powered algorithms can personalize search results based on individual user preferences, search history, location, and other factors. This personalization enhances the user experience by delivering more relevant and tailored search results.

Voice Search and Virtual Assistants: AI plays a crucial role in voice search and virtual assistant technologies. Voice-activated devices, such as smart speakers and voice-enabled smartphones, utilize AI algorithms to understand and respond to user voice commands, providing hands-free search experiences.

Algorithm Updates: Search engines continuously refine their algorithms using AI to improve the accuracy and relevance of search results. Updates like Google's BERT algorithm, which focuses on understanding natural language, demonstrate the increasing influence of AI in shaping search engine behavior.

User Experience and Engagement: AI algorithms consider user engagement metrics, such as click-through rates, bounce rates, and dwell time, to assess the quality and relevance of search results. This helps search engines refine their rankings and prioritize content that generates positive user experiences.

Image and Video Recognition: AI algorithms can analyze and understand visual content, including images and videos. This enables search engines to deliver more accurate results for visual searches and offer relevant video content.

Continuous Advancements: As AI technology continues to evolve, search algorithms are expected to become even more sophisticated in understanding user intent, providing personalized recommendations, and delivering highly relevant search results.

As AI continues to advance, search algorithms will become more adept at understanding and meeting user expectations. It is crucial for website owners and SEO practitioners to stay informed about AI-driven advancements in search algorithms and adapt their strategies to align with the evolving landscape. By understanding the role of AI in search algorithms, businesses can optimize their online presence and improve their visibility and relevance in search engine results.

IX. Case Studies: Successful Evergreen SEO Strategies

Real-World Examples Of Websites Benefiting From Evergreen Algorithms

There are numerous real-world examples of websites that have benefited from evergreen algorithms, resulting in increased visibility, organic traffic, and overall success. Here are a few notable examples:

Wikipedia: Wikipedia is a prime example of a website that leverages evergreen content. With its vast collection of information on a wide range of topics, Wikipedia's articles tend to provide comprehensive and timeless information. Due to its focus on high-quality, evergreen content, Wikipedia consistently ranks highly in search results and attracts a significant amount of organic traffic.

HubSpot: HubSpot, a leading marketing and sales software company, has established itself as a reliable source of evergreen content in the field of digital marketing. Their blog and resource library feature in-depth articles, guides, and tutorials that remain relevant and valuable over time. This focus on evergreen content has not only helped them build authority in the industry but also drive consistent organic traffic to their website.

WebMD: As a popular health information website, WebMD creates evergreen content that addresses common health concerns, symptoms, and treatments. By providing accurate and reliable health information that remains relevant over time, WebMD has positioned itself as a trusted resource. This has led to increased visibility in search results and a substantial organic traffic volume.

Moz: Moz, a well-known company in the field of search engine optimization (SEO), has built its reputation by consistently producing evergreen content that educates and empowers SEO professionals and marketers. Their blog, guides, and tools provide valuable insights and actionable advice that remain relevant in an ever-evolving SEO landscape. As a result, Moz has gained a strong online presence and attracts a large audience of SEO enthusiasts.

Food Network: The Food Network website offers a wealth of evergreen content in the form of recipes, cooking techniques, and food-related tips. The website's focus on timeless content has made it a go-to resource for cooking enthusiasts, resulting in high search engine rankings and a steady stream of organic traffic.

These examples highlight the benefits of creating and optimizing evergreen content. By focusing on topics and information that remain relevant and valuable to users over time, these websites have established themselves as authoritative sources in their respective niches. Their consistent traffic and visibility are a testament to the effectiveness of evergreen algorithms in driving sustained online success.

Analysis Of Their Strategies And Implementation Techniques

Wikipedia:

- Strategy: Wikipedia's strategy revolves around providing comprehensive and reliable information on a wide range of topics. They focus on creating evergreen content by ensuring that their articles are well-researched, properly cited, and regularly updated.
- Implementation Techniques: Wikipedia employs a community-driven approach, where users contribute and edit content to maintain its accuracy and relevancy. They also follow strict guidelines for content creation, including neutral point of view and verifiability, to maintain the quality of their articles.

HubSpot:

- Strategy: HubSpot's strategy involves producing valuable content that addresses the needs and challenges of their target audience in the digital marketing field. They create comprehensive guides, tutorials, and case studies that offer actionable insights and solutions.
- Implementation Techniques: HubSpot focuses on thorough research, expert contributions, and visual elements to enhance the value and readability of their content. They also optimize their articles for search engines by conducting keyword research and including relevant keywords naturally within the content.

WebMD:

- Strategy: WebMD's strategy revolves around providing accurate and trustworthy health information to their audience. They cover a wide range of health topics, from common ailments to complex medical conditions, ensuring their content remains relevant over time.

- Implementation Techniques: WebMD employs a team of medical professionals and experts to review and validate their content. They emphasize medical research, authoritative sources, and expert opinions to ensure the accuracy and credibility of their articles. They also optimize their content for search engines by including relevant keywords and providing helpful meta tags and descriptions.

Moz:

- Strategy: Moz's strategy is centered around educating and empowering SEO professionals and marketers. They produce content that covers various aspects of SEO, including industry trends, best practices, and data-driven insights.
- Implementation Techniques: Moz uses a combination of research, data analysis, and industry expertise to create their content. They conduct original research, perform case studies, and share real-world examples to provide valuable and actionable information. They also optimize their content for search engines by targeting relevant keywords and ensuring their articles are well-structured with headings, subheadings, and bullet points.

Food Network:

- Strategy: Food Network's strategy is focused on providing a wide range of recipes, cooking techniques, and food-related content that appeals to cooking enthusiasts. They aim to create content that is accessible, informative, and enjoyable for their audience.
- Implementation Techniques: Food Network focuses on visually appealing content by including high-quality images, videos, and step-by-step instructions in

their recipes. They optimize their content for search engines by including relevant keywords, clear titles, and well-structured content. They also encourage user engagement by allowing users to leave comments, rate recipes, and share their experiences.

Overall, these websites implement their strategies by prioritizing quality, relevance, and user experience. They conduct thorough research, leverage expert knowledge, and optimize their content for search engines to ensure maximum visibility and engagement. By consistently delivering valuable and evergreen content, they have established themselves as trusted sources in their respective industries.

Lessons Learned And Actionable Takeaways

Quality and accuracy are key: The success of websites benefiting from evergreen algorithms stems from their commitment to delivering high-quality and accurate content. Prioritize thorough research, expert contributions, and authoritative sources to establish credibility and gain user trust.

Regular updates and maintenance: Evergreen content requires ongoing updates and maintenance to ensure its relevance and accuracy. Implement a process to review and update existing content regularly, keeping up with the latest industry trends and information.

User-focused approach: Understand your target audience's needs, preferences, and search intent. Create content that addresses their pain points and provides valuable solutions. Optimize your content for user experience by improving readability, incorporating multimedia elements, and enhancing engagement factors.

Keyword optimization: Conduct thorough keyword research to identify relevant keywords and phrases that align with your content and audience. Incorporate keywords naturally throughout your content, including headings, subheadings, and URLs, to improve search engine visibility.

Build authoritative backlinks: Focus on acquiring high-quality and relevant backlinks from reputable sources. Guest blogging, influencer outreach, and building relationships with industry experts can help attract valuable backlinks to your site.

Monitor performance and analytics: Utilize SEO analytics tools, such as Google Analytics and Search Console, to track your website's performance, keyword rankings, organic traffic, and user behavior. Use this data to identify areas for improvement, make data-driven decisions, and optimize your SEO strategies.

Stay updated with algorithm changes: Keep a close eye on search engine algorithm updates and industry trends. Stay informed about the latest changes and adapt your strategies accordingly to maintain and improve your website's visibility and rankings.

Prioritize user experience: Invest in mobile optimization, fast page load speeds, and intuitive website design to enhance user experience. A user-friendly website that delivers a seamless browsing experience can positively impact engagement metrics and overall search engine rankings.

Create comprehensive and engaging content: Develop in-depth, well-researched, and engaging content that goes beyond surface-level information. Incorporate visual elements, multimedia, and interactive features to captivate and retain user attention.

Foster user engagement and social signals: Encourage user-generated content, social media sharing, and community engagement to create a buzz around your content. Actively participate in discussions, respond to user comments and feedback, and leverage social media platforms to amplify your reach.

Remember, the world of SEO is constantly evolving, so it's essential to adapt and refine your strategies as needed. By implementing these lessons and actionable takeaways, you can enhance your website's visibility, drive organic traffic, and establish a strong online presence.

X. Conclusion: Embracing the Evergreen SEO Mindset

Recap Of Key Insights And Best Practices

- Evergreen algorithms prioritize high-quality, relevant, and user-focused content.
- Regular updates and maintenance are crucial to keep content fresh and accurate.
- Keyword optimization helps improve search engine visibility and relevance.
- Building authoritative backlinks from reputable sources boosts website credibility.
- Monitoring performance and analytics provides valuable data for optimization.
- Staying updated with algorithm changes ensures ongoing optimization.
- User experience should be a top priority, including mobile optimization and fast page load speeds.
- Comprehensive and engaging content attracts and retains user attention.
- User engagement and social signals contribute to search engine rankings.
- Utilizing SEO analytics tools helps track performance and identify areas for improvement.

By following these key insights and best practices, you can create a strong foundation for your SEO strategy and increase your chances of success in the ever-changing digital landscape. Remember, SEO is an ongoing process, so continue to adapt, refine, and stay up-to-date with the latest trends and algorithm updates.

Encouragement For Long-Term, Sustainable Seo Efforts

Embarking on a journey of SEO requires dedication, persistence, and a long-term mindset. As you navigate the ever-evolving landscape of search engine algorithms and digital marketing trends, it's important to stay committed to your SEO efforts and embrace the following encouragement:

Patience is key: SEO is not an overnight solution. It takes time for search engines to recognize and reward your efforts. Stay patient and consistent in implementing your SEO strategies.

Focus on quality over quantity: Instead of chasing quick wins or shortcuts, prioritize creating high-quality content, building authoritative backlinks, and delivering an exceptional user experience. These sustainable practices will yield long-term results.

Stay updated and adaptable: SEO is an ever-changing field. Keep up with industry updates, algorithm changes, and emerging trends. Adapt your strategies accordingly to ensure your website remains optimized and competitive.

Embrace continuous learning: SEO is a dynamic field with new techniques and tools emerging regularly. Invest in ongoing learning to enhance your skills, stay ahead of the curve, and maintain a competitive edge.

Test, measure, and iterate: Implement tracking and analytics tools to monitor the performance of your SEO efforts. Analyze the data, identify areas for improvement, and iterate your strategies accordingly.

Seek guidance and support: Don't be afraid to seek guidance from SEO experts, join communities, and participate in discussions. Learning from others and sharing experiences can provide valuable insights and support.

Celebrate milestones and progress: SEO is a journey, and every milestone achieved and progress made deserves celebration. Recognize and acknowledge the fruits of your labor, no matter how small, as they contribute to the bigger picture of long-term success.

Remember, sustainable SEO is about building a solid foundation, maintaining best practices, and adapting to the evolving digital landscape. With perseverance and a commitment to delivering value to your audience, your efforts will be rewarded with improved visibility, increased organic traffic, and long-term success. Keep going, stay resilient, and embrace the ever-changing SEO landscape with enthusiasm and determination.

Embracing Ongoing Learning And Adaptation To Algorithmic Changes

In the ever-evolving world of SEO, staying ahead of algorithmic changes is crucial for maintaining and improving your website's visibility. To effectively adapt to these changes, it's important to embrace ongoing learning and keep up with industry updates. Here's how you can do it:

Stay informed: Regularly follow trusted industry blogs, forums, and news sources that provide insights into algorithmic changes and SEO best practices. This will help you stay updated on the latest trends and developments.

Engage in continuous learning: Invest time in expanding your knowledge and skills through online courses, webinars, workshops, and conferences. Learn about new SEO techniques, tools, and strategies that can help you navigate algorithmic changes.

Join SEO communities: Engage with other SEO professionals and enthusiasts by joining online communities, forums, and social media groups. Participate in discussions, ask questions, and share your experiences. Learning from others can provide valuable insights and different perspectives.

Experiment and test: Algorithmic changes often require adjustments to your SEO strategies. Embrace a culture of experimentation and testing. Try out new techniques, track their impact on your website's performance, and make data-driven decisions based on the results.

Analyze and adapt: Regularly analyze your website's performance using SEO analytics tools. Monitor changes in rankings, organic traffic, and user engagement metrics. Identify any negative impacts from algorithmic changes and adapt your strategies accordingly.

Focus on user experience: Search engines are increasingly prioritizing user experience in their algorithms. Stay attuned to user behavior trends and align your website's design, content, and navigation to provide a seamless and engaging experience.

Embrace white hat SEO: Instead of resorting to black hat techniques that may provide short-term gains but lead to penalties in the long run, focus on ethical and sustainable SEO practices. Build high-quality content, earn authoritative backlinks, and prioritize user satisfaction.

Leverage data and insights: Use SEO analytics tools, such as Google Analytics and Search Console, to gain valuable data and insights into your website's performance. Monitor keyword rankings, click-through rates, and conversion metrics to make informed decisions and optimize your strategies.

Adapt to user behavior shifts: As user behavior and search trends evolve, adapt your content and SEO strategies accordingly. Keep an eye on emerging technologies, such as voice search and mobile usage patterns, and optimize your website to meet these changing user preferences.

Embrace a growth mindset: SEO is a dynamic and ever-changing field. Embrace a growth mindset that fosters curiosity, resilience, and a willingness to adapt. View algorithmic changes as opportunities for growth and improvement, rather than obstacles.

By embracing ongoing learning and being adaptable to algorithmic changes, you position yourself for long-term success in SEO. Continually educate yourself, analyze data, test new strategies, and prioritize user experience to stay ahead of the curve and maintain a competitive edge in the digital landscape. Remember, staying agile and adaptable is key to thriving in the ever-changing world of SEO.

www.ingramcontent.com/pod-product-compliance
Lightning Source LLC
Chambersburg PA
CBHW070443220526
45466CB00004B/1759